40 THE YEAR OF NA... DANGEROUSLY

YOUR GUIDE TO LIFE ON THE OTHER SIDE OF THE HILL

ILLUSTRATED BY: BILL BRIDGEMAN

TURNING 40: A HISTORICAL PERSPECTIVE

GEORGE WASHINGTON AT 20:

"I CANNOT TELL A LIE."

TEDDY ROOSEVELT AT 20:

"SPEAK SOFTLY AND CARRY A BIG STICK."

HARRY TRUMAN AT 20:

"THE BUCK STOPS HERE".

WASHINGTON AT 40:

"I CANNOT TELL A JOKE WITHOUT FORGETTING THE PUNCHLINE."

ROOSEVELT AT 40:

"SPEAK UP AND INTO MY GOOD EAR."

TRUMAN AT 40:

"MY BACK HURTS HERE."

3

TOP 10 REASONS IT'S BETTER TO BE 40 THAN 20

10) PUTTING ON LOOSE-FITTING CLOTHING SAVES PRECIOUS MINUTES EACH MORNING.

9) RESTRICTED DIET REDUCES ANXIETY WHEN ORDERING LUNCH.

8) NO MORE NEED TO WORRY ABOUT SILLY DREAMS OF "MAKING YOUR MARK."

7) IF YOU'RE UP AT 2 A.M., IT'S FOR A REASON.

6) NO MORE TIME WASTED WONDERING HOW TO FIX HAIR.

5) RESEARCHERS IN MALLS DON'T BOTHER PEOPLE WHO ARE OBVIOUSLY WALKING FOR THEIR HEALTH.

4) NOT DRIVEN TO RECKLESS ACTS OF PASSION BY HORMONES.

3) EASIER TO BE A GREAT BRIDGE PLAYER THAN A GREAT BASKETBALL PLAYER.

2) HAVING A LIST OF DOCTORS' PHONE NUMBERS IN YOUR HEAD SAVES TIME IN EMERGENCIES.

AND THE NUMBER ONE REASON:

1) LOTS CHEAPER TO JUST GAZE OUT THE WINDOW AND SIGH THAN TO TRY TO ENTERTAIN YOURSELF WITH THINGS LIKE MOVIES, CONCERTS AND DATES.

AT THE BIRTHDAY PARTY

A FEW SIMPLE RULES WILL HELP MAKE YOUR 40TH BIRTHDAY PARTY SAFE AND ENJOYABLE. JUST REMEMBER:

1) AVOID STANDING TOO CLOSE TO THE CAKE. THOSE EYEBROWS TAKE FOREVER TO GROW BACK.

2) IF A PACKAGE IS LARGE, DON'T TRY TO PICK IT UP AND SHAKE IT. (REMEMBER YOUR 'CONDITION'.)

3) BEFORE BLOWING OUT THOSE CANDLES, NONCHALANTLY TRY TO MANEUVER YOUR CAKE TO A POSITION NEAR A LARGE FAN.

COMPLIMENTS 40-YEAR-OLDS MOST LIKE TO HEAR

THE 40-YEAR-OLD'S RULES OF THE ROAD

1) "WHEN IN DOUBT, HIT THE BRAKES."
2) "WHEN NOT IN DOUBT, HIT THE BRAKES."
3) "THE TURN SIGNAL SHOULD BE USED AT LEAST THREE BLOCKS PRIOR TO THE TURN."
4) "IF SOMEONE BEHIND YOU WANTS TO PASS, THAT'S JUST THEIR TOUGH LUCK."
5) "USE THE SIDEWALK ONLY TO AVOID POTHOLES."

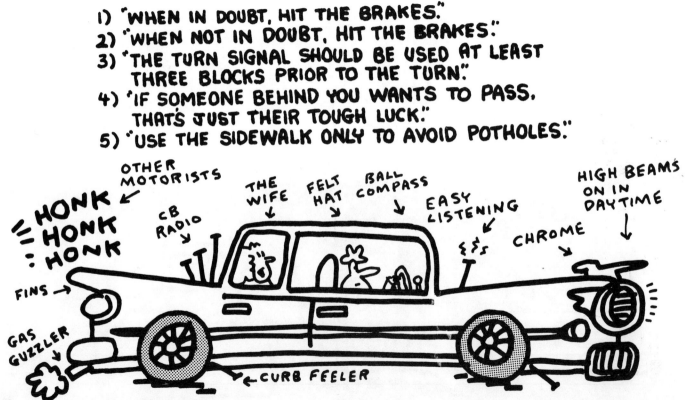

the ideal lover

THE REQUIREMENTS PEOPLE LOOK FOR IN THE IDEAL LOVER CHANGE AS WE GROW OLDER. HERE ARE SOME OF THOSE REQUIREMENTS FOR THREE SPECIFIC AGES:

AGE 18: A SEXUAL DYNAMO.

AGE 30: SENSITIVE AND ATTENTIVE.

AGE 40: BREATHING.

EXCITING NEW PRODUCTS FOR THE 40-YEAR-OLD!!

FASHION TIPS: COVERING THAT GRAY HAIR:

THE "HOLD-UP" LOOK

"DOWNHILL RACER"

"THE KING AND YOU"

THE "ARMCHAIR QUARTERBACK"

WHICH DOG IS 40?

DAY 1   DAY 2   DAY 3

FOR THE 40-YEAR-OLD: THE "KING FORMULA 40" GRADUALLY AND IMPERCEPTIBLY RESTORES HAIR TO ITS NORMAL COLOR AND FULLNESS.

THE BODY AT 40

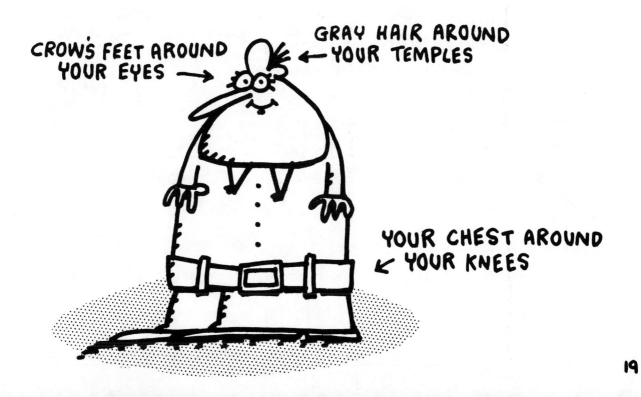

THE 40-YEAR-OLD MEAL PLAN

ROMANCE NOVELS FOR THE 40-YEAR-OLD

WHAT PEOPLE SEE IN THIS DRAWING

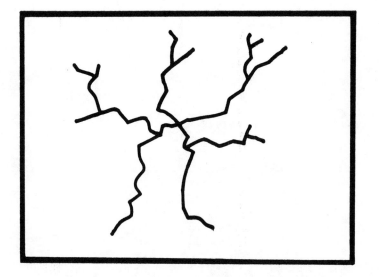

18-YEAR-OLD: WINDOW PANE BROKEN DURING A SOFTBALL GAME.
30-YEAR-OLD: ROAD MAP OF HIGHWAY SYSTEM.
40-YEAR-OLD: YOUR LEG, BEFORE PANTYHOSE.

GREAT POTENTIAL MOVIE ROLES FOR THE 40-YEAR-OLD

1) NEW HOME OWNER WITH A MYSTERIOUS CURSE

2) MAN RESPONSIBLE FOR OIL SPILL

3) HOLLOW TREE

LAUGHING HYENAS AT 40

WHERE THE MONEY GOES: A COMPARISON

$ $ $ $ $ $ $ $ $ $ $ $ $ $ $ $ $ $ $

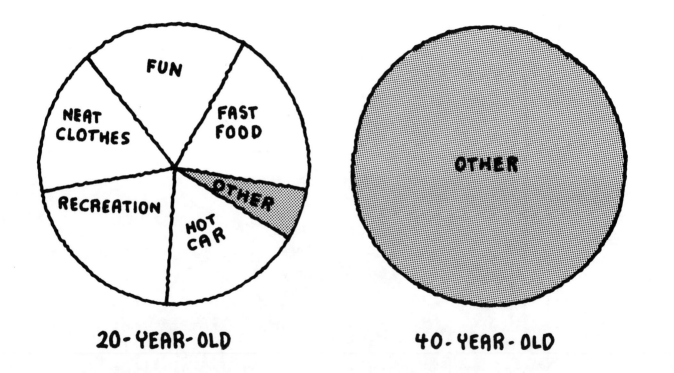

20-YEAR-OLD   40-YEAR-OLD

OUR CHANGING HEIGHTS

JANE AT 20   JANE AT 40

the 40-year-old workout

THE EXERCIZE MOTORCYCLE

THE ORTHOPEDIC FLOOR MAT

THE "OVER-THE-HILL" TREADMILL

"LAXATIVE"

THE MEDICINE CABINET STRETCH AND REACH

SPLASH

THE "WITH THE CURRENT" ROWING MACHINE

30

FASHION TIPS, PART II

HOW TO HIDE THOSE FIGURE FLAWS

1) BUY LOOSE CLOTHING.

2) BORROW LOOSE CLOTHING.

3) ACCEPT GIFTS OF LOOSE CLOTHING FROM FRIENDS AND RELATIVES.

THE TOP 10 COMPLAINTS
OF THE 40-YEAR-OLD BOWLER

10) EYESIGHT MAKES FOR AWKWARD 10-10-7-7 SPLIT.

9) SIXTEEN-POUND BALLS SEEM A WHOLE LOT HEAVIER THAN THEY USED TO.

8) BEVERAGES-TO-BATHROOM RATIO DECLINING FAST.

7) NO MULTI-COLORED VINYL BELTS TO MATCH BOWLING SHOES.

6) LANES STAY OPEN LONG PAST YOUR 7 P.M. BEDTIME.

5) YOUNG PUNKS WHO ARE ACTUALLY ABLE TO JUMP OFF FLOOR WHEN THEY MAKE A STRIKE.

4) WHEN STANDING, CAN'T TELL IF BOWLING SHOES ARE TIED.

3) FOOT-LONG CHILI DOGS NOT ACTUALLY A FULL FOOT LONG, AS IN GOOD OLD DAYS.

2) FOUR-STEP APPROACH ACTUALLY REQUIRES TAKING FOUR STEPS.

AND THE NUMBER ONE COMPLAINT:

1) PEOPLE KEEP TRYING TO BOWL WITH YOUR HEAD.

CLASSIC NOVELS FOR THE 40-YEAR-OLD

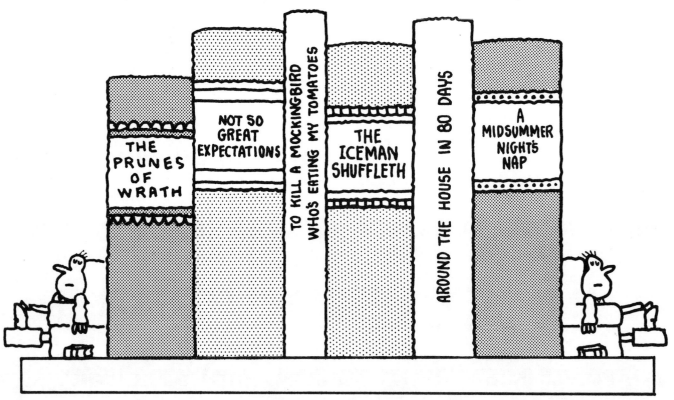

GREAT INVENTIONS FOR THE 40-YEAR-OLD

THE SEE-HEAR-AND-SMELL GLASSES WITH OPTIONAL HAIR-PIECE ATTATCHMENT

RIDDLES, RIDDLES, RIDDLES

Q. WHAT DOES A 40-YEAR-OLD DO IF HIS HAIR BURSTS INTO FLAMES?

A. THROW IT ON THE GROUND AND STOMP IT OUT.

Q. WHAT DO YOU CALL A 40-YEAR-OLD WHO TOSSES AND TURNS ALL NIGHT, HAS BAD DREAMS FROM INDIGESTION, AND WAKES UP IN THE MORNING WITH STIFF MUSCLES AND AN ACHING BACK?

ZBLUG SHBLUH ZERK

A. GRATEFUL FOR THE "WAKES UP IN THE MORNING" PART.

Q. WHERE WOULD THE 40-YEAR OLD SEE THE MOST WRINKLES: IN FIVE DOZEN PRUNES, OR ON A RELIEF MAP OF THE SOUTH DAKOTA BADLANDS?

Q. HOW DO YOU SPOT THE 40-YEAR-OLD IN A GROUP OF JOGGERS?

A. NEITHER. SHE'D SEE THE MOST WRINKLES AT A CLASS REUNION.

1) HAS AN AMUSING GAIT DUE TO HEAVY ACE BANDAGING.
2) IS BREATHING LIKE A RUNAWAY TRAIN.
3) IS CLUTCHING AN AREA PEOPLE DON'T USUALLY CLUTCH IN PUBLIC.

AT THE OFFICE

WE'VE REPLACED THE 40-YEAR-OLDS' COFFEE WITH INSTANT DE-CAF. LET'S SEE IF ANYONE NOTICES...

DREAMS AND THE 40-YEAR-OLD

DREAM: YOU ARE BEING CHASED BY TURKEYS.

MEANING: JOB INSECURITIES. YOU FEAR BEING PASSED OVER FOR A PROMOTION.

DREAM: YOU ARE WALKING DOWN A BUSY STREET NAKED. NO ONE SEEMS TO NOTICE

MEANING: YOU FEAR THAT YOU ARE NO LONGER AS ATTRACTIVE AS YOU USED TO BE.

DREAM: YOU ARE UNABLE TO BECOME INTERESTED IN SEX.

MEANING: YOU ARE AWAKE. TRY TO GET SOME SLEEP.

THEME PARK

KNOCK OVER THE MILK OF MAGNESIA BOTTLES

GUESS YOUR BLOOD PRESSURE AND CHOLESTEROL

THE 40-YEAR-OLD GOES FISHING

A COMPARISON: WHERE PEOPLE GO TO HEAR SOME REALLY HOT MUSIC

18-YEAR-OLD: A DANCE CLUB DOWNTOWN.

25-YEAR-OLD: A BAR DOWNTOWN.

30-YEAR-OLD: A NIGHTCLUB DOWNTOWN.

40-YEAR-OLD: AN ELEVATOR DOWNTOWN.

ELASTIC MAN AT 40

COMMON SEX FANTASIES OF THE 40-YEAR-OLD

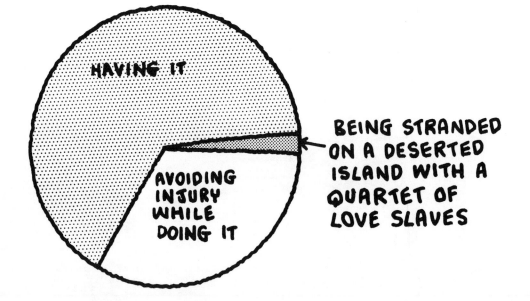

HAVING IT

AVOIDING INJURY WHILE DOING IT

BEING STRANDED ON A DESERTED ISLAND WITH A QUARTET OF LOVE SLAVES

GO FOR THE  BURN

NOW THAT YOU'RE 40, THIS PHRASE PROBABLY IMPLIES:

1) EXERCISING UNTIL YOUR MUSCLES ACHE.

2) WALKING UNTIL YOU START TO CHAFE.

    OR MORE LIKELY...

3) FALLING ASLEEP UNDER THE HAIRDRIER.

A 40·YEAR·OLD GOES ON VACATION!

1) FALSE TOOTH BRIDGE
2) LAKE INFERIOR
3) MOUNT SLEEPMORE
4) ST. LOUIS FALLEN ARCH
5) ASTRO-CHROMEDOME
6) KIDNEYSTONE NATIONAL PARK
7) THE GREAT NO-SALT LAKE
8) BRAN CANYON

Memories

NOW THAT YOU'RE 40, YOU MAY START TO REMINISCE ABOUT THE THINGS YOU DID AS A CHILD THAT YOU CAN NEVER DO AGAIN, INCLUDING:

1) CHASING AFTER THE ICE CREAM TRUCK ON YOUR BIKE.
2) FALLING ASLEEP IN THE BACKSEAT AS YOUR DAD DRIVES HOME.
3) TOUCHING YOUR TOES.

A 40-YEAR-OLD'S DREAM HOUSE

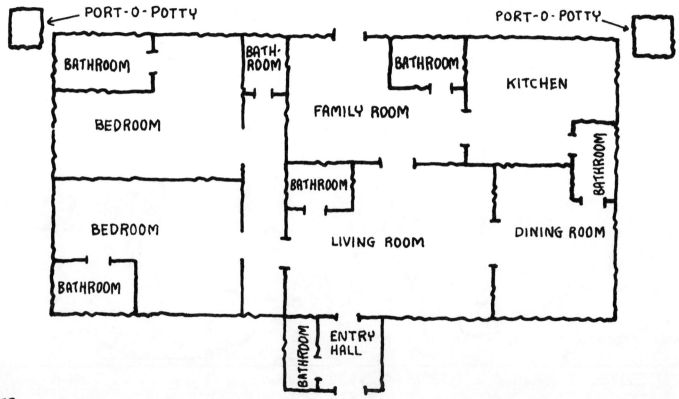

OPTIONS FOR THAT CAR

THE BIFOCAL WINDSHIELD: NEVER AGAIN WILL YOU HAVE TO WEAR THOSE UNSIGHTLY GLASSES WHILE YOU DRIVE.

BRING BACK THOSE LAZY, HAZY, CRAZY DAYS...

96 FM

THE RADIO LOCK: TO ENSURE THAT YOUR RADIO NEVER STRAYS FROM YOUR FAVORITE "EASY LISTENING" STATION.

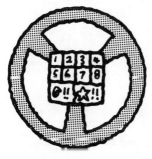

THE PROGRAMMABLE HORN: INSTEAD OF THE SIMPLE "HONK!", THIS HORN CAN BE PROGRAMMED TO SHOUT, "GET OUT OF THE WAY, YOU LOUSY PUNK!"; "PICK IT UP... I'VE GOT AN APPOINTMENT WITH MY CHIROPRACTOR!"; AND THE EVER POPULAR, "LEARN TO DRIVE, PAL!"

A 40-YEAR-OLD'S TOP 10 FAVORITE SONGS

10) LET'S GET A PHYSICAL

9) AIN'T NO BURRITO MILD ENOUGH

8) JOHNNY B. OLDE

7) HOW DO YOU MEND A BROKEN EVERYTHING?

6) THE LACK'A MOTION

5) HAIR POTION NUMBER NINE

4) DOCTOR MY EYES (AND EARS AND JOINTS AND BACK AND...)

3) TO ALL THE GIRLS I'VE DISAPPOINTED BEFORE

2) A HARD DAY'S NAP

1) KNOCK, KNOCK, KNOCKIN' ON THE BATHROOM DOOR

An OPTICAL illusion

WHICH WHITE PATENT LEATHER BELT IS LONGER?

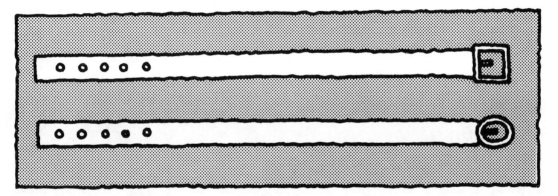

ANSWER: THEY ARE THE EXACT SAME LENGTH! EITHER ONE WILL EASILY HOLD UP ANY SIZE 50 PANTS!

POPULAR PICK-UP LINES OF THE 40-YEAR-OLD

"I PROBABLY WON'T BE AROUND LONG ENOUGH TO KISS AND TELL".
"WANT TO LOOK YOUNGER? HANG AROUND WITH ME!"
"TIRED OF SEXUAL PARTNERS WHO KEEP YOU AWAKE ALL NIGHT?"

59

FUN SCALE FOR THE 40-YEAR-OLD

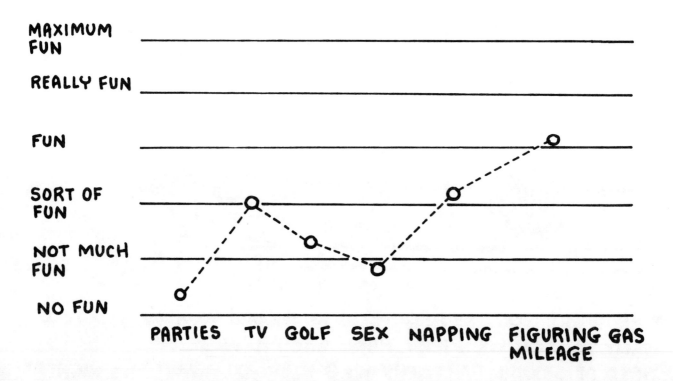

TOP 10 PET PEEVES OF THE 40-YEAR-OLD

10) TOILET PAPER THAT FAILS TO LIVE UP TO
SOFTNESS CLAIMS.

9) CHOLESTEROL NUMBER TWICE AS HIGH AS I.Q.

8) WHAT 40 CANDLES DO TO THE SURFACE OF A CAKE.

7) BIG DOGS WHO JUMP UP AND DON'T CARE IF THEY
KNOCK YOU DOWN.

6) REALLY HEAVY DICTIONARIES.

5) SUPPORT HOSE THAT DOESN'T EXACTLY MATCH SKIN COLOR.

4) ALWAYS THOUGHT GINGIVITIS WAS A FOREIGN TENNIS PLAYER.

3) TALL CURBS.

2) LIMITED COLOR SELECTION OF THREE-WHEEL BIKES.

AND THE NUMBER ONE PET PEEVE:

1) SWIMSUIT CALENDARS THAT DON'T HAVE HOLIDAYS LABELED.

the changing you

NOW THAT YOU'RE 40. IT'S TIME YOU ACCEPTED THREE FACTS OF LIFE:

1. YOUR SHOT AT WINNING A DECATHALON IS BEHIND YOU.

2. YOUR CHANCE TO MAKE YOUR FIRST MILLION BY AGE 30 IS BEHIND YOU.

3. AN ENORMOUS BUTT IS BEHIND YOU.

three views of a tub of water

THE OPTIMIST'S VIEW: HALF-FULL.
THE PESSIMIST'S VIEW: HALF-EMPTY.
THE 40-YEAR-OLD'S VIEW: "COULD YOU HEAT
IT UP A LITTLE AND ADD SOME EPSOM SALTS?"

Famous Fairy Tale Characters at 40

HOW WILL YOU LOOK WHEN YOU'RE 40?

(JUST TURN THIS PICTURE UPSIDE DOWN!)

TRICKS 40-YEAR-OLDS TEACH THEIR DOGS

FAVORITE CLASSIC MOVIE LINES OF THE 40-YEAR-OLD

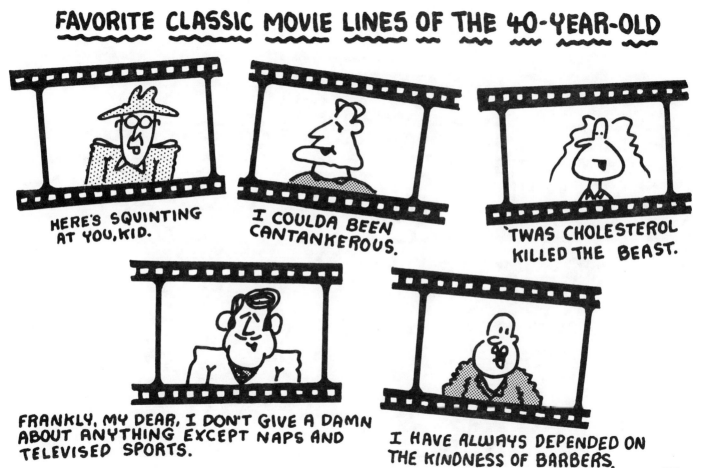

HERE'S SQUINTING AT YOU, KID.

I COULDA BEEN CANTANKEROUS.

'TWAS CHOLESTEROL KILLED THE BEAST.

FRANKLY, MY DEAR, I DON'T GIVE A DAMN ABOUT ANYTHING EXCEPT NAPS AND TELEVISED SPORTS.

I HAVE ALWAYS DEPENDED ON THE KINDNESS OF BARBERS.

CHEERLEADERS AT 40

WRITTEN BY: CHRIS BRETHWAITE
BILL BRIDGEMAN
BILL GRAY
ALLYSON JONES
KEVIN KINZER
MARK OATMAN
SCOTT OPPENHEIMER
DAN TAYLOR
RICH WARWICK
AND
MYRA ZIRKLE

Books from:

SHOEBOX GREETINGS

(A tiny little division of Hallmark)

STILL MARRIED AFTER ALL THESE YEARS
DON'T WORRY, BE CRABBY: Maxine's Guide to Life
40: THE YEAR OF NAPPING DANGEROUSLY
THE MOM DICTIONARY
THE DAD DICTIONARY
WORKIN' NOON TO FIVE: The Official Workplace Quiz Book
WHAT... ME, 30?
THE FISHING DICTIONARY
YOU EXPECT ME TO SWALLOW THAT? The Official Hospital Quiz Book
THE GOOD, THE PLAID AND THE BOGEY: A Glossary of Golfing Terms
THE CHINA PATTERN SYNDROME: Your Wedding and How to Survive It
THE GRANDPARENT DICTIONARY
STILL A BABE AFTER ALL THESE YEARS?
CRABBY ROAD: More Thoughts on Life From Maxine
THE HANDYMAN DICTIONARY A Guide For the Home Mess-It-Up-Yourselfer